# INVITATION TO KIM

# BOOKS BY GEORGE SCARBROUGH

## POETRY

*Tellico Blue*
*The Course Is Upward*
*Summer So-Called*
*New and Selected Poems*
*Invitation To Kim*

## FICTION

*A Summer Ago*

# George
# Scarbrough

# INVITATION
# TO KIM

Edited by

Phyllis A. Tickle

## IRIS PRESS

Distributed by
Peachtree Publishers, Ltd.

Memphis • Atlanta

1989

Typography by Patterson Publications, Inc.

ISBN -0- 918518-71- 7
$14.95

THIS BOOK IS ALSO FOR DALE

The Town          outsider,
Tenantry          but not alien


Mill n the Chestnut
Early   Autumn
Excursion
Gumption
   Last Look—Winter Break—Summer Revised
Grace


The Sharer
A Family Fable

Summer
A Death in the Family
Sonnet for My Brother Lee
        The Game
Leather
Daddy, You Bastard

Implication

Invitation to Kim
The Mantlepiece
Mutiny, Bedbug
Life Line   The Mantlepiece
Morning Day
   Winter Break
   Summer Revised
Bedbug
Plowing
Vacation

   My Grandfather Said
   Schoolhouse Hill
   Night Mill

# CONTENTS

II.
OF COURSE THE PLACE IS SMALL . . .

III.
PUT THE BOOKS ON THE FLOOR . . .

IV.
THE WAY A MAN HANGS . . .

## Editor's Note

In the spring of 1988 I began the editing of *Invitation to Kim*, a volume which was as elusive at times as it was assertive of its own integrity. I had, the poems said, only to listen to them in order to expose the nexus which bound them to each other and to the canon of Scarbrough's work. Now, well over a year later and with my task complete, I know that the poems spoke truthfully.

There are sixty-two volumes of Mr. Scarbrough's previously unpublished letters, notebooks and journals which are now assigned to Iris Press. Only a small percentage of such largess could be included here; the rest awaits editing for future publication.

I trust that after you too have encountered *Invitation to Kim*, you will join me in the keenest anticipation of that event.

Phyllis A. Tickle

# ON READING SCARBROUGH

George Scarbrough was the first poet I ever knew.

I can remember no formal introductions but simply, in the student manner, the easy, sporadic bursts of exchanged confidences about tastes and texts in the wide corridors of Ayres Hall, where we joined a dozen others assembling for our University of Tennessee classes in Shakespeare, Browning, or Poe. In our class in Herman Melville (we were unaware of just how up-to-date Nathalia Wright was in offering an entire seminar devoted to the recently recanonized author), while I struggled with the murkier segments of the transcendentalized *Mardi*, my classmate George, understandably as I later discovered, tackled Melville's poetry. I remember little about his report, a dutiful analysis of Melville's ragged prosody and truncated metaphysical imagery, but his informal, passionate summary sticks firmly in my mind: Melville was a better poet in his prose than in his poetry. Though over the years I have come to change my opinion (and perhaps George has, too), at the time all of us had to agree with this poet's judgment of another poet. What better authority about such matter than a practicing poet? Though more than a handful of us thought of ourselves as potential writers, here was the real thing.

By the time I knew George Scarbrough as a flesh-and-blood poet, I had already taken a course called "Modern Poetry" and, thanks to the patient ministrations of Robert Daniel and his chosen text, *Understanding Poetry* (the squat blue original of 1938), I had been steered to isolated poems by Yeats, Auden, Frost, Eliot, Hart, Crane, Allen Tate, E.E. Cummings—and Joyce Kilmer. Only after I knew Scarbrough the fellow student did I actually know Scarbrough the poet. I bought *Tellico Blue* and read it with great pleasure—but mostly with the shock of revelation. I still occasionally consult its now-smudged pages with their faint vertical lines penciled in the margins—not that I think that first book is the best of Scarbrough, but to return to *Tellico Blue* is to remember the joy of surprise, the stab of familiarity in seeing how someone I knew could transform what then passed as prosaic figures and landscapes of my own place into compelling art. Robert Penn Warren has recorded a similar suffusing pleasure and awe when he was first a student of John Crowe Ransom: here, he marvelled, was a man who had actually published a volume and who was using people and places he too had always known.

To my knowledge, in the subsequent forty years no new Tennessee talents and titles flowered from our classmates' experience of *Tellico Blue* in quite the same way as the Nashville poets flourished in the wake of *Poems About God*. But in my files I yet preserve a draft of my only effort at substantial fiction, a much-revised, still-bad novel called "Hymn for the Sound of Hymns"—the title a tribute to what was once my favorite poem from *Tellico Blue*. It is not Scarbrough's best, even in that first volume, but its testy, poignant dismay, its affection-frustrated exasperation, fueled my own creative and emotional engine in 1950.

As my academic career took its desultory course, i continued to read Scarbrough: mostly the succeeding volumes, *The Course Is Upward* and *Summer So-Called*, but occasionally in the little magazines where some of their entries first appeared. In the hiatus from 1956 to the early 1960s I lost all track of George Scarbrough, though for a college composition anthology in 1966 I remembered and introduced my coeditors to a remarkable prose preface to *The Course Is Upward*, a plangent memory piece called "Several Scenes from Act One" that later proved to be a superb classroom text for students deficient in the preception of tone. In the 1960s also I occasionally noted with pleasure a Scarbrough poem in *Sewanee Review*—by now the journal I most regularly read. But not until 1977, with he publication of *New and Selected Poems*, did I catch up with the fine mature work of George Scarbrough. Here were poems in which the rich subjects of previous years were rendered even richer by a mode and manner that plunged far beyond the comforting couplets and sonnets of the early verse. It was a precise poetic style whose line was relaxed but controlled, with idioms ranging from vernacular bluntness to elegant wordplay and with cadences that accommodated narrative situations as well as lyrical evocation. Above all, the emotional range was spectacularly, nakedly, human: philosophic, erotic, grief-ridden, raging, bitter, resigned. Perhaps a shadowy autobiography could be reconstructed through *New and Selected Poems* (especially if we reckon into the record *A Summer Ago*, a fictionalized account of a pre-adolescence boy growing up in Scarbrough country), but the enduring value of his work reaches beyond and behind a life actually lived—into that realm that art makes available to others, strangers and friends alike, who have their own lives to live. In one of his prose pieces, Scarbrough ponders the superiority of nonverbal communication over words— words are, as he puts it, "the least exigent in message"—and yet even there he appreciates the paradox that even that pertinent observation must come to us in words. "Reading is the rede to follow," as he says more than once.

And now we come to the latest Scarbrough.

*Invitation to Kim* might be subtitled "You Come Too." Beautifully structured, the book is built on the extended metaphor of the house as self. It is at once Scarbrough's most honest and most appealing volume. The range is narrower than in *New and Selected Poems* only because there is no poem here that celebrates rage in quite the flamboyant and virtuoso way of, say, "Madness Maddened." Perhaps because the pervasive consciousness of age threads its way throughout the book, the poems celebrate instead the serenity of confidence, but with nary a trace of

xvi

complacency. The serenity of these poems has a bite, an energy churned up by the exacting eye ("watching/My hand raisin with age") and the intellect that continues to glory in the delight of puns and wordplay— which he himself attributes to "My love of the profligate/Word." The sustaining intricacy of "Early Autumn" (governed by he image of communal knife-sharpening), the witty vignette of "Bedbugs" (whose generative core is the linkage of *scald-scold-skald*), the transformation of painful childhood experiences into usable values through verbal magic in many poems, but I particularly think of "Tenantry" ("Always in transit/we were always temporarily/ in exile . . . . It was the measurable/ pleasurable earth/ that was home"): this volume aggressively submits the self that experiences, that remembers, to prying eyes that are also invited to be loving; but that submission has a stylish playfulness, even in its somber moods, as if to say: the mind that suffers can also redeem. The vehicle of that redemption is the word.

"He knew his very bone was boundary," a line from an early poem, anticipates the movement and substance of *Invitation to Kim*. Against the single image of dispersal—the wagonwheels moving to and from a succession of interchangeable tenant houses—is ranged a solid accrual of sites proud in their fixity: coves, streams, knolls, rooms, rootcellars, pastures, graveyards, angles of land, and, the dominant image, the poet's house: "I never wanted/ More than comfort/ Of a close fit: snug/ Door, low ceiling:/ Approximations of a/ Warm embrace." Scarbrough's boundaries are thus fixed in the geography of lower East Tennessee, but a "riverine brain,/ On whose topography the mind/ Is so tremulously posited" permits him voyage to extend, absorb, and challenge the predictability of consolation that regional place all too often invites. As he says in one poem, "Things last in/ Unexpected ways." One of these things is the wound of family that refuses to be totally healed by the salve of memory. Both physical geography and relational topography are crowded with father, mother, brothers—a clangor of attitudes unsentimentalized by the necessary affections of age.

In Scarbrough's only novel, A *Summer Ago*, is preserved—unshaped by false dramatic action—that relational topography in which boyhood is gridded by the perspective of maturity: "The boy finds in his father his beginning and periphery, and in his mother his center and circumference; and these dimensions from point to outpost, are the universe." Cross-hatching of perspective clarifies, but it does not falsely console, the nag of affectional ambivalence.

*From point to outpost:* George Scarbrough's universe is capacious enough to accommodate us all and restrictive enough to make us feel the pinch.

—James H. Justus
Indiana University

xvii

# INVITATION TO KIM

# HISTORY

Sifted through England
On the way to Pennsylvania,
They came out of the Danelaw.
The record is set in my father's
Proud, high-prowed face.

I, English toned and tainted,
With Bucks County only a name
Like a kite at the end of a long
Thread in a cold northern sky,
Do not plan to go there.

Somewhere South through
Sweetbriar, Knox, Anderson,
Roane, to Polk, the Cherokee
Dropped in for a chat, leaving
My father such cheekbones!

They almost crowd his eyes
Shut in the old photograph (prow
Merely augmented). The Dane shows
Still in the way his head rides
His neck like a tall ship.

Scarborough (North Sea) Scarbrough,
Scarberry is the way the name goes,
Traceable on landholds: *a fortified
Place*. In the Danelaw: *Skarthi's fort*,
Ramparts apparent still

In the formidable look.
The other (Celtic) essence of me
Sounds in my mother's highland name:
McDowell: son of the dark stranger.
Sept, not clan. Perhaps

1

Explained by the swarthy son.
Sifted through Ireland on the way
To Cape Hatteras (fleeing rejection),
They came eventually to mountains.
On the way a red-haired Dutch

Girl dropped in for a chat,
Leaving my mother her auburn hair.
It was the color of a stormcloud
Besieged by sun.  In the photograph
It reddens like dawnlight.

Daughter of the wandering
Medical Scot, she crossed (at age 2)
The last western escarpment, dropping
By jolt wagon down to Tennessee,
Polk County, and my father,

Errant orphan she would later
Marry mostly from pity, she said.
But it was not a pitiful marriage,
Grim poverty notwithstanding.
She was the driving force.

Dying, he cried, "Some water,
Please," adding the word "home."
One hand under his head, with the other
She held the cup steady, returning
It full to the kitchen.

Leafing again the worn album
(Bachelor on a Sunday afternoon,
With whom avoidlessly the line stops),
Pondering the long treks they
Took to my native county,

These folks of mine,
Bringing me rich blood and certain
Not negligible gifts (acknowledged now
In far places), I am perplexed
To be the one to subvert history.

2

# INVITATION TO KIM

This is the house
That George built
Of fetched-together
Fragments of father-
Made harm, mother-
Minded weal, sibling-
Sized obloquy, cousin-
Crossed odium, and
All the kudos of
The great-aunt kind.
Dear youngest one,
Born too far along
In the astral flights
Of a Christmas season
To affect my house
With anything but love,
Please come in.

Of course the place
Is small. I never wanted
More than comfort
Of a close fit: snug
Door, low ceiling:
Approximations of a
Warm embrace. Is it
So depraved, in one who
Took so readily to
Praise, to want so
Much to be enfolded?

Put the books on the floor.
These chairs are never
Sat in. Clear a place
On the table for the prized
Cup, and take care when
You walk the narrow paths
Of this house. Reading

Was the rede I followed,
Finding in the letter
The spirit that escapes
The law.  I make no apology
For weak eyes and a certain
Effeminacy of manner.
Books engender the
Androgyne: a fact our
Father was quick to note.
His demeaning name for
Me still burns my cheeks
With the flush of deep shame.

The reason for the
Boxes should be evident.
They are the hasped
And hinged covenants
I am secure in.  Are
Extensions, likely, of
Half a bureau drawer.
By the time you arrived
Among the assorted houses,
There was no longer need
To fractionalize the
World's goods into
Components of seven.

As for the peacock
Feathers sweeping the
Ceiling from the top
Of the highboy, do not
Be disturbed by their
Extravagant glances.
Juno had such eyes.
Such ocular regalia
For a man's bedroom
Does not, however,
Compromise the ultimate
Seemliness of his bed.
Is it such an unforgiveable

Offense to be so plumed
In ordinary adversity,
Even though we were taught
From the beginning
The pejorative nature
of love?

Knowledge is the other
Name I chose for love,
Though there are doubtless
Other fitter names
For other fitter men.
Come in, dear Kim.  Come
In.  Beauty is the utmost
Grace of knowing, and I
Have posited this house
Upon the lean, glazed
Stones of grace.

The way a man hangs
A blue hat on a yellow
Wall, and makes an art
Thereby, is, after all,
The way an art grows
In official clothes
To guard a cornfield.
That I choose now
To stuff a greater abstract
Does not make me a strange
Being by virtue of my
Other vices.  I know you
Hide your canvasses in
A closet, not knowing
I know.  We were share-
Croppers, Kim.  Come in
Now, and share.

Askance is always asked
For, Brother.  Come in.
We will strip the walls

Of their immoderate
Orchestral sound, and
From the morningglory
Mouth of the beautiful
Gauche machine will pour
The same implausible music
Of fiddles wobbling in
The air, at whose thin
Snarl of plangency, we
Stood, smiling our round
Heads off, in that other
House uphill, before we
Learned our evening meal
Of bread and other
Country accoutrements
Could be so entertained
With violins.

There are annals here
You are much too young
To be aware of.
Mother is here, in any
Room, wearing a cherry-
Bob hat and tatting a
White skullcap for her
Adoring son, the genius she
Thinks she will not have.
I surmise in my incorrigible
Intent, that on his red
Hair, when he appears,
The netted headstall will
Be as the red veins in
His pale, quite monstrous
Brain.  There is no red
Hair in my family,
Beyond the Dutch grandmother,
That I know of.
Certainly, neither of us
Is cousin to that
Human vermillion. Yet

We are all we are.
I am freak enough only
To imagine the freak among us
Genius would have been.

Forgive the conceit.
Metaphor is, at worst,
The least baneful of
My vanities, though I know
My love of the profligate
Word has always been a
Wearisome point with you.
You could never understand
My cheerful proneness
To furnish out the least
Analogy over the discouraging
Fact. I wear an aura of
Palpable lies. I have
Entertained that suspicion
Myself. But how little,
Little Brother, fact
Analogizes the world it
Too nicely trims the
World to.

It is, of course, only
An adopted habit of mind.
Too engrossed in convoluted
Things to think straight,
I am, as it were, engulfed
By corals, cabbages, and
The deep hearts of cyclonic
Flowers, as well as the
Swirls and eddies of the
Humped, riverine brain,
On whose topography the mind
Is so tremulously posited.
Forgive me, please.

Look.
Through the door to
The next room, father,
The great disapprover,
Looks in, making a stain
Of ebony and red against
The farther wall, himself
Epitome of the beauty he
So thoroughly despised
In his own sons.
A troubled air diffuses
About him but not today
Reaching his round,
Chestnut eyes, for the time
As meaningless as the old
Brown doorjamb he leans
Against. With him, it is
Always something about out-
Comes, a measure of harvests,
And this has been a pleasantly
Gravid year.

I, in ways his son
Twice-over, bring you to
Him through a beautiful autumn
Door.

This, then, is my
Checkered dwelling, Kim,
My piecemeal place.
Patched with ghosts a close
Celebration wraps me in.
All things are signed here
With the personal graffiti
Of love. Guardian spirits
Swarm all over the old
Furniture. Under Dan's
Water-blue mountain, Rob's
Heron flies eternally to
Rest on the inkstand,

Kinsman not, as usual,
Of the consanguineous kind.
Love, too, is happenstance,
Though such interiors as
Mine are not as accidental
As they seem.

Come in, Brother.  Because
I love you, I have spent my
Life trying to teach you
Two things:  How to let a
Brother live as he will
And die his own way:
Two things which are only
One in the end.  We are old now.
Must I still plead my obstinate
Case with you?  Let us once
More share the thin gleanings.
In the presence of painted
Ladies, old souls, and tribal
Laser eyes, who can say what
Is the best nature
Of love?

## I

*Of fetched-together*
*Fragments of father-*
*Made harm, mother-*
*Minded weal, sibling-*
*Sized obloquy, cousin-*
*Crossed odium, and*
*All the kudos of*
*The great-aunt kind.*

# A FAMILY FABLE

Once there were 3
x 3 Bares
Papa Bare
Mama Bare
And Seven Little Bares
who lived in several
houses in
several woods
for several years

but never long
nor never twice
in the same wood
because Papa Bare
though really quite an
amiable sort
had Several Defects in
Attitude
including a very
short temper
which he would
invariably
show off to the Great
Big Bear
who ruled whatever wood
the 3 x 3 Bares
happened to be living
in at the time

and for his
temperamental
pains
would get sent packing
with the other eight Bares
down the road
they had just come up
looking for another
wood to settle in

going along
the 3 x
3 Bares laughed
in the jolt wagon
as if they were
picnicking
on Kool Aid and
ham sandwiches

Mama Bare would be
telling the story
how she would ask
just how with
all this going
about the world
will Little Old Goldilocks
no matter how many
butterflies come by
her gate
ever catch up to
our poor porridge
and plump her behind
on the hard bench
behind our long table

(at the thought of
the heartless little
entomological house-
breaker's potential
callouses
Papa Bear would cluck
to his team
and lean back and
snap his galluses)

Mama Bare would laugh
and go on with the story
as for sampling the beds
she said
to try the lot
the girl would have to come
for the whole summer
besides
it's spoken around

that the truant young miss
is somewhat remiss
in vocabulary
having skipped so much
word study at school
from running around
the neighborhood
chasing commas
question marks
and painted ladies

Mama Bare would giggle
at the idea
*too high at the head*
*too high at the foot*
*too hard*
*too soft*
and all that *just*
*right* business
(imagine!)
wouldn't do
no siree
she'd find all the beds
considerably sagged
in the middle
from sheer Bare weight
and too high at both ends
that would put a bend
in her bundle
and boggle her bolster
excellent turns of phrase
if I do say so myself

here
Mama Bear would giggle again
and paw her bosom
in ample self-
satisfaction
while the Seven Little
Bares all
sniggered together

as for getting along
with her sampling

she said
the girl would find herself
stuck in the first bed
on the fourth pillow
as I have foretold
not being good
the poor dear
at synonyms
antonyms
and all those other nyms
so necessary to
the furnishing out
of the bare body
of perfect utterance
any of you could
have done much better
from hearing the language
spoken so well
at home

Mother Bare would purse
her lips into Pure
O
her favorite sound

and so the 3
x 3 Bares
mimicking sandwiches
would all laugh heartily
together again
and go on down the big
road to another house
in another wood
where Papa Bare would soon
bare his terrible
temper
to the Reigning Bear
of the Wood

(who just wouldn't be
cussed out)

and
along with the other Bares

get sent packing once more
up the road they
had just come down
looking for a new place
to settle
Mama Bare still telling
the story

and all of them laughing
like Bares bare of reason
because they knew that
until
the flighty little
lepidopterist
found her way to their house
the tale could never
be ended

# THE GAME

Up the hill in the landlord's house
The small boy in suit with collar
Played backgammon with his mother
In the room where the rockinghorse stood
White as a morning cloudbeast
Behind the white gauze curtain.
Selling blackberries, in my rough clothes
I beseeched a ride:
"That rig would play hell
With the paint job," my father said.
So are introductions made,
Accommodations learned.
At our house we played hell.

About the rockinghorse there was no dispute.
I could see I was not properly attired
For consorting either with fine beasts
Or collared boys.
And when my astonishment was over,
I accepted the rules proposed by the master
Of revels, whose sumptuous eye
Contained both hell and heaven
In a glance, though he seldom
Blandished heaven.
Hell was nearer country, lying contiguous
With his presence.
"If hell is his game," my brother said,
"By hell, I mean to play."

In whatever book my brother read,
I read assiduously.  And so
We studied total gamesmanship
Under his caustic observation, projecting
Appropriate landscapes in the air
Of searing attribution he provided.
Once, out of sight in the fields,
We tried to play hell all by ourselves
And found it didn't go, and ended up
By spinning round and round,

Our arms outspread,
Dipping and singing:
"Now we're playing hell!
Now we're playing hell!"
Until we dropped, dizzy as hell,
Onto the hot ground and laughed ourselves
To sleep.
Heaven was, thus, the mote
In his absent eye.

Up the hill they toyed with clear
Civilities.  At our house we practiced
Smokier paradigms, stubborn as hidden fire
Under an old stump, making a win
Of wonderment and despair.
Oh how the captain grinned
In hateful disbelief at the small,
Prodigious player who sank the axe
Into the chopping block up to the eye.
And when the handle came away
In the player's hand:
"Now you've played hell!" the captain said.
"Look who's calling the signals now!"
My brother carolled,
Graduated and proud.

Little tenuous, unsullied steed,
The curtain bellies out in this old room,
And I see behind the thin white net
The sweet round body I could not saddle
With my knotted crotch because
I would have marred your hide.
Mad, I sit before the windy window and sing:
"Blackberries, blackberries!  Oh who
Will buy my rich, ripe berries
That I may come in out of the hot sun?"
Adept now at my father's game,
Master of more revels than he ever was,
I wonder, untouchable, dearest beastie,
Would there have been a difference
Had I been fit to ride?

# MY GRANDFATHER SAID

My grandfather said:
Never climb a tree too high
to get back down
before dark.
A tree at night is a foreign country.
You don't speak the language.
And your hands can't talk
for you after sunset.
You'll be caught up there
among those roadways
that crook and cross,
those leaf-hidden houses,
those tittering strangers,
and not know whether
the way they advise
will lead you home
or merely elsewhere.
How could they find up-ness
in their speech for
a phrase to tell you
what is merely down?
Because they are foreign,
they act without mercy.
It's no fault of their own.
So spake grandfather.

Take my advice.
Never trust a grandfather.
There's nobody up a tree
but you, if you do.
All that muck about roads and houses
and people that talk a foreign language
was purely grandfatherly shit.
All I learned is
that night doesn't fall.
It comes from the ground
like black smoke rising.
And there I sat,
thinking to follow

the last light down
from the other direction!
and hollering like hell
for him to come
and bring a flashlight.
And all the while,
at the top of the tree,
a green-gold flag waved black and silver
and a whippoorwill called
so cold and lonesome,
I pissed my pants
while he was getting there.

# LEATHERS

I'm ten, and my behind is being honed
By my father's razor strap, the rasping
Behind me like the sound of breath going
Out and in: *wish swish wish swish,*

Until I am brought to a fine edge,
Not of tears but of the wonderful thought
That I love leathers: straps, thongs,
Rawhides to tie with, up, down, and

Together. Reins, too, and girths,
Leashes and whips (ah, whips!),
Checklines and bellybands. The string
In my pocket still smells of skin.

It is my most precious possession.
Soon I will have a valise of leather,
Soon I will go away in a leather coat.
I will write a poem, too, and bind it

In leather. But for now my father hones
My behind: *wish swish wish swish.*
I look up into his leathery face.
Excitement gathers in my loins.

# GUMPTION

After a summer of trial and error
(It had to be error for we tried hard),
Ignoring grubs, bubbling lures, puckering
His kissy mouth at us dangling down
From the fallen-tree bridge,
Uninterested in September as in April,
Old Gump still rose and fell
Like a humpbacked sun
In the blue turn of the creek.

Conceding first, Lee abandoned his post
To prowl the banks, threshing a track
Through tangled brakes to try
Less famous holes.  The last soggy
Pill of dough sailed away,
The naked hook, black in the paler
Water, crooked like a beckoning finger.
I drowsed, the game exceeding its charm.
Cool as shaded cucumbers, the sun
Rolled down like a harvest wagon.

At my brother's word I came alive
And lifted a line straight up as a plumb,
Exposing a lump of gold lazily finning
The moted air.  I yelped in unbelief.
This was not the way it should have been.
Angrily, I tried to shake the arbitrary
Thing back into the water.

But Lee came running rattling summer's end.
"Goddam, what a fish," he screeched,
Oblivious of the propriety of ways
And means, absorbed in lovely ends.
"Goddam," he yelled again, exulting,
Plowing the shallow like a herd,
Bug-eyed as bait.
Snatching the pole from me, he danced
A victory dance (as after skill and courage)

At the edge of the corn.  I had gone numb
At the inconsequence of things,
The tasteless indifference.

Going home I followed,
Lee cavorting ahead.

## EXCURSION

On that coronal day of the week,
Deferring Sabbath School,
I stowed my book in the haymow
And took the path to the dam.

The river eddied past,
Wearing a transfer of willows;
Trailing rosespots in decrescent
Lines, a trout swam past

The imaged leaves.
Well up the river now,
I considered cornsnakes poked to anger,
Yards of hissing color.

The sun rose past the first
Bell call.  I ducked my head and spoke
My verse quickly, "Jesus wept,"
And then again quickly

As if nobody had heard,
And plodded on, the green objective
Rising just ahead, the sloping
Earthwork of the dam,

Topped with a fret of stone,
From whose height I meant to take
The sun's height at the height of noon.
But from the pinnacle

I saw them coming:
Slithering conclave considering
Concert:  cottonmouths twisting like
Thick arms in heavy sleeves.

A musty fume rode the hot air.
Black on stone, brown where the sun
Strafed the slathered grass,
Gray in trampled mud,

They came on and on.
My heart squeezed shut like an empty
Paper bag. My feet stuck in the dead
Pace of dreams.

The converging rough things
Held me in a ring, the gaping mouths
Like faded bogland roses. I leaned
And vomited in the dirt.

When my eyes cleared, they were gone,
As if at signal. My feet came loose.
Gulping my own sour slobber, I ran
As runners do who bring a message home.

# THE MILL ON THE CHESHUA

*(for Seamus Heaney)*

Sacks of ivory corn stood straight or lurched
Along floorboards, lacking community muster.
Bins of tick-fat wheat amassed the sun's gold
Where shafts of light whirled with motes of flour.

Other gear than grain's decked the floor,
Smooth and hollow-sounding over the vast piled cavern
Underneath. Through cracks the sunshafts pierced
The nether gloom, lustering great mealy webs.

From July to autumn the wheel shook the shore:
Bright shovels danced, forks shivered on their tines,
Collars whinnied without horses. I practiced keeping
That musty middle world strictly at eye-level.

But eyes went up irresistibly to the ledge
Where, stood on end and leant against the wall,
The coffins were the cynosure: plain pine kits
Of the miller's offhand skill, of various sizes

Like families talking together. Gulping
One last lung-full of the treacherous bread,
I scuttled into the yard, into the starveling light
Of trees and broken millstones and brown water.

Chaffy birds flashed in the sun. Whitened myself,
I lay face-down in the grass, refusing to turn over
To front the fear above. That would have made it easy.
The grainy coffins moved in like thick-armed elders.

# EARLY AUTUMN

On Saturday the grindstone turned
At the community's eye. Their arms piled
With dull knives, hands full of whetstones,
The old croppers came, hunkering,
Spitting a dark, oily spittle.

The grindstone could run a man dry.
All morning it waded the trough, flung water
Like the leading edge of a universe unwinding
Itself. Father and son took the stone
For crosscut saw and mower blade,

Axe and scythe. I, being son,
Was loaned around. Being an old cropper
Guaranteed nothing but being an old cropper.
The lyric abrasion sounded till noon,
When the bright knives, filed, were

Filed away. There were terse farewells.
The old croppers, stiff-lipped, hawked dust.
The circle loosened, drifted. A fricative note
Still hung in the well-honed air.
*Wish, swish, wish swish* went the wind.

Laid out with professional care,
Fine edges gleamed in every household.
The fields were prime for cutting. Grasses
Nodded, rich in corners. Behind railings,
Pigs watched with blue intelligent eyes.

28

# VACATION
(For Rebecca)


A clumsy valve
Loose in its chamber
Or a muffled hammer

Halved of its helve,
With rage and clamor
The old churn worked

Mechanic mad
Till scalded milk's
Volcanic boil

Yielded the plunger's
Capricious ramble
An even motion

Slubbed as silk,
And frog-spawn rounded
The plunger's back:

Masses of spittle,
An egg, an oil,
An eye, a tittle

In the lessened clack:
And water squeezed
Back to the churn

As pirning eased
To easy turn
And butter came

In dappled seethe
Of sweating cream
Like a summer island.

## SONNET FOR MY BROTHER LEE

Our mother said, "He makes a dunce of you,
That brother of yours.  Why will you play his fool?"
I had sat atop the pasture gate for him
To try his sling, whether his aim was off
Or true.  His aim was true.
And I went bawling home to her dispraise.
Another time he cajoled me into jumping
The orchard wall into a heap of dung
He knew was there for me to land in.
I ran stinking home to announce his sin.
She whipped him for that, eliciting promises,
Which were always made to be broken, he said,
Chortling.  I never learned to distrust him wholly.
Loving him, I loved being his fool.

## MOVING DAY

Eleven,
and in his father's powerful opinion
man enough now for the job,
he carried the knotty sea-conch
that contained the sea-boom:
inexplicable family treasure
come from God knew where
outside the county garden.

Tilting it carefully
so that the tides it held
would not spill out into the hogtrough,
he sat in the back of the wagon
among the pitchforks and ploughs,
his bare feet salted with cold
under his numb ass,
his ear pressed to the creased
and sunrise pink of the slit
his brother likened to quite another thing—
much to his younger shame.

He knew from the book
surreptitiously hidden
under the folds of an old quilt
that what he heard was the sound
of his own blood running its salt tides,
aggrandizing pulse acoustically recorded
against itself in the shell's rooms.

But such knowledge was not yet fashionable
in the home county.
Nonetheless, now and then,
passing the glassy roadside trees
clacking their heads together,
he stole a look at a wet page.

Once when the wind was right,
in a time of great decision,
half-animal flowers stood up

from their cooling salt rocks
and walked with the tide
onto the fire-baked shore,
the book said.

Something of hearsay.
Something of heresy.
He listened again to the shell's
pulsating roar.

His father's,
the sea monster's,
shoulders rose before him in the milky mist
like an island cliff he moved toward
always the same distance away.
The mules stepped smartly on
down the hard clay road,
their job being set
to step smartly on
regardless of the sea horses,
sea cows, sea calves
looming alongside
in winter pastures.

And so they came to the house
next on the agenda,
where dead hollyhocks sighed in the yard
and a creeping vine writhed on the doorway.
A glazed brown pigeon perched on a windowsill.
A ragged crow peered down
from the cold chimney-top.

When he stood up happy
on his bloodless, sat-on feet,
both book and shell slipped from his ebbing hands.

"I'll burn that goddamned book
the minute I light a fire,"
his father, the beached dirt farmer,
howled backward into the blasts
of icy November wind
beginning to sweep down over miles
of red county land,
booming *home, home.*

# DADDY, YOU BASTARD

Daddy, you bastard,
when you were angry,
your black brows dived together
like two hawks swooping down
on the same prey:
poor, whimpering rabbit-boy,
luminous-eyed fool
trusting in the efficacy
of short grasses.

Daddy, you bastard,
you always wore your hat
when you whipped me
as if to formalize the event.
I thought if I
could hide your hat,
you would not beat me.
But firstlight, lastlight,
your hat was always clamped
on your raven head.
How could I get at the top
of your watchful tower?

Daddy, you bastard,
I remember your hands most of all
holding a match flame
in a gray winter wood
the day your dinner came late.
I loitered at the holly tree
bleeding its deep scarlet heat
into the milky air,
and then I ran until
the dishes rattled.
But I was late.
Your hands were golden,
bone-streaked cups of wrath.

Daddy, you bastard,
you gave me a toy once:
a little tin pail with a spade
and Old King Cole on its side.
I did what was natural.
I carried dirt into the house
to please you.
Old King Cole was a merry
old soul, but,

Daddy, you bastard,
You were not amused.
I traded your gift for a red ball
And got another whipping.
With you I could never win.
I grew up in a striped suit,
Hating you for the longest
Childhood on record.

Too short on love too long,
I am still short on love.
It would please you to know,
Daddy, you bastard,
That I never exceeded
The cut of my clothes.

## LAST LOOK

Leave a coin in a chink
a marble in the runnel
of an eave
a plate on a shelf

not the best you have
something you will miss
but can do without
a coat hanger

wound with bright
threads will do
a flowerbox
with live roots in it

perhaps a towel
frayed but usable
washed clean
on a nail behind

the kitchen door
pack well for the moving
take a long last
look

in closet and drawer
leave nothing unsought
but that you seek
to leave

in the swept house
tidy as sunlit
Sunday
something for the finder.

# THE SHARER

*(For my father. An exercise poem*
*after Seamus Heaney's "The Servant Boy")*

Old work-whore,
Cherokee slave blood
Manumitted
To serfdom:

Free to choose master
Yet bound to be chosen,
Roving the county
In annual unchoosing:

Wintering-out
Each new year
In a new place
With an eye to autumn

And moving on:
Hunter-gatherer,
Blood-bearer,
Rabbit-shoe man:

Resentful,
Impenitent,
Among strange outhouses
Swinging his lantern,

He draws me after him
Into his broken trail
From sty to stall,
To stack,

Stithy, and beyond
To the big houses where
I see him stand,
Tugging no forelock,

Amiable and dangerous,
At front doors accosting
The little landlords
For his share.

36

# THE MANTELPIECE

On the mantelpiece
Carnival glass vases
Flank the fake foxed clock.
The clock has scabbed
In the leak of time
Though it was once gold
And brown like mixed marble.
The vases are blue what time
They are not purple and violet.
They suggest the peacocks
The landlord keeps
To decorate his garden.
With the clock they achieve
A classic balance
Though nobody knows that.
The clock has balance, too:
Grooved columns flank its face,
Suggesting doorposts
To a round portal
Round things might enter:
An owl's hole.
Largely speaking the time
The clock keeps
Is one hundred and one.
The tall oil lamp
At one end of the smoke-
Black board is at a loss
For balance.  It has
A Greek-key bowl
Though nobody knows that,
And its light is like an egg-yolk.
What the lamp doesn't balance
With is the conch at
The other end of the board.
Leached bone-color
Its rhinoceros hide
Has heaved and heaped
Coming two hundred years
By jolt wagon inland

From Cape Hatteras.
Truncated, its crest makes
A mouth to be trumpeted,
Summoning home.
I have heard it curling.
Even in egg-yolk light
Its fan, upheaved,
Is still sunrise pink above
The gray lambrequin,
Which might be imagined the sea.

It has no history beyond
A series of grandmothers.
It is there in the blank cabin
Among the dry wilds
Of Tennessee cedars
Because someone (nobody
Can tell who)
Cared to carry it there.

The vases verged by flamelight
From purple towards gold;
The shell raised a morning sky
For the landlord's birds
To cry in, their wail
A shudder in the scalloped light
The lamp's knot faded to.
But it was the clock that
Was sovereign in the house.
Behind its leaved Corinthian
Columns the raw clay
Of the chimney rose
Like a matrix from which
It had emerged, rubbed free
By what it measured,
To stand forth in all
Its templar distinction.

What else there was behind us
In the room we did not know.
We sat craning forward
Into the fire and upward
To the precious stone
On the mantelpiece.

# SUMMER REVIVAL: BRUSH ARBOR

He preached a sermon, wild and wonderful.
His word's improbable beauty brought us down

To wallow gorgeously before him in the brown
Brush of his summer church.  Outside, the dull

Land blazed, with nothing ever beautiful:
A monotone on hill from foot to crown.

His word's improbable beauty washed it down.
An epic vision broke the summer's lull.

Under his eloquence, we seemed to drown,
Becoming souls, though quick and animal

In all our joyous parts, from foot to crown:
Being a soul is also beautiful.

And soul and body brimmed up to the full
When his improbable beauty brought us down.

# WINTER BREAD

In my mother's kitchen
The meal bin
Was a fine oak barrel
With stout staves and
Scrubbed brass bindings,

By all odds the best
Furniture in the house
In its corner
At the head
Of the long table.

My mother dipped
Her head in, dipping,
Straightening
With a scoop
Flaked and spilling

Back rough bran
That smelled of old
Whiskey and popped corn.
Fruit-jar bouquet.
I begged permission

To dip my head in,
And she allowing,
Came up ineluctably
Drunk with
The yeasty atmosphere.

How bright the hoops,
Evenly stacked on darkness,
Shone in the half-
Light from the stove.
I could hear,

Outside,
The wolf-wind
In the valley.
It was December.
It is again December.

The wolf-wind howls
In the valley.  This
Is a comfortable house,
With certain not-
Plain appointments,

(Among the best
Of furniture there is
No best furniture),
But there is nothing
I would not forego

To lift again
The lid of the meal
Barrel in my mother's
Kitchen for one deep
Unreconstructable

Breath
Of winter bread.

41

# THE WELL

Twelve, and fit for casements
No man could enter
(What dream ever again so close?),
I, tethered, swung down
To sweating darkness,
Dangling lantern glow
Past rotted beam,
Perched salamander,
Wet black stone
To the scrag run of bottom water.

The wide-eyed face leaned
Intimately to mine,
Head against my shoulder,
While I roped and bound
And signaled and let go
With arms upraised,
Wanting back for company
The young dead wife who,
Rising, took the light:

Than whom no other was
Ever more dreadly accosted:
For whom I could have shrilled
Accusations from the stygian pit,

Whose far eye winked and opened.
The tackle, coming, creaked.
Hurrahing haulers,
Jubilant at contest where none was,
Handed me up to the wellhead,
Immense noonlight,
And the rough declaration
Of gratulatory hands.

And to another man's incredulous,
Dry-eyed blasphemy:
"Christabitch.  Christabitch."

# POEM FOR WILLIAM OSCAR

Cupped to light
my morning fire
the brown bones bend

in the thick, flushed fingers
as on a thousand mornings.
The flame arouses,

and he turns to say:
*your bread and milk
are ready on the table.*

*Arise and shine,*
his sad, salad face—
retinal image in russet

and raw tomato red—
riding high in the room's gloom.
He stands at the foot of my bed.

It is always the same.
Through the bare window we can see
the white stones appearing

on the beechwood hill
as the last pale stars fade
like tongued-out gold flowers

in a lapped-up blue saucer.
The blue is overbearing now,
taking all the stars except one

that glows low among the bushes
and stones over a stone
white as beehives or snow.

Then his face floats free,
sharp as singeing mineral
to any cloudy shape.

Under tight-crushed lids
I squeeze the vision out of my eyes
and go to cup and plate,

eating elusive fragments,
drinking ungettable compounds,
in my hesitant breakfast joy

(which is always, dear father,
only as measured as the moment
love is assured).

# BEDBUGS

### I

Was it an interloping briar,
An extraneous nettle,
Pricking me, the ticking gone sharp,
Thorny nest wound in the new straw?

What bur, I wondered, inquisitor
Of the burning thigh.

To realize suddenly
What my hands were so
Avidly crushing—
Warm fat round rubies—

And to stand and rush,
Sweating my own blood,
Into the moonlit porch.

### II

In the new house not new
But newly moved into,
The beds were unhinged again
And hauled into the air,
It following that what was here
Was there.

They leaned in their pieces
Against the palinged fence.

A scar of moon was still in the sky,
Pale paring of light.

Then my mother strode forth,
Indignant to the roots of her hair.
"Squatters," she said. "Trash,"
Heaving buckets of scalding lye water
Onto the smoking frames.

45

From the head of the great oak bed
Carved oak leaves fell, melted
From their mooring.
Varnish sluiced away.

The posts stood up white
As cactus bones in the morning sun.

Her hands seemed bags of weariness
Exploding again and again.
Scald, scald, scald.

Then, in the rooms,
Hot water curled up walls to the ceiling
And whitened down.
We took sharpened sticks and scraped
The sodden chinches from the cracks.

"Vagrants," my mother scolded. "Scum,"
Indignant to the roots of her hair.

### III

Words, I wondered, inquisitor
Of my parboiled room,
Thinking *scald*, thinking
*Scold*, thinking *skald*:

Old horned mystic rhymer
Who doused an errant folk
With scalding mouthfuls of words
To rid them of the larval things
Infesting their own epic system.

The dictionary gave me dreams.

Under a minikin moon,
Thin peeling of October light,
I lay on my ghostly bed
And waited for dreams to bite.

# SUMMER

The ungainly rabbits posed and waited
In the desert for the thirteen-year-old
Who killed his age in a morning.

The blood-shot summer he gave me!
When the porous flesh sealed its doors
Against all but scarlet exudations!

The blood-clot summer he bequeathed!
Geysered, leaped, whispered, cascaded
That summer!  But I loved him no less.

I even carried a gun to be like him,
Ostensibly for snakes, nudging the dry
Bush for the awakening I had no hope for.

How have explained the difference
Beyond hot and cold had the opportunity
Come for the gun?  To myself, I mean:

Because of what runs in the sun
With awkward, deft explanations of fire,
Ice is also a pattern, a passion all its own.

Among the pink and white jellies, those
Candied shapes, the yellow wax of flowers,
The blood poured and seethed, the morning

Leaped like the horse at the cold,
Inscrutable, sliding maculation
Of the snake I sought far not to kill.

Resourceful as I am, I had no answer
To bestow between the tick-infested, sloe-eyed
Innocence of the one and the other's power,

Had my gun been upped in his eyes'
Demand for the proving of myself
In his joyful pastime.
A season had me close by the heart,
Closer by the head, and would not let
Me go, no, not even for his love.

# SCHOOLHOUSE HILL

At the noon hour
She traipsed townward
To steal the creams and sticks
She bought her friends with:
From her coats and cuffs
Spilled the economies of love.

Past love's savagery,
Larceny left her.
Abandoning contraband,
She drifted about Benton,
The metropolis of all our lives,
In pleasant rue.

Uphill again she flourished
In perfumes like bouquets,
Sweetened by her own sack:
Then, butterflies in sight,
She dropped down again
Into the yielding town.

I stole too for my moment
Of attractiveness. Pariah
Of ordinary hours, I stuck
To my desk at noontime, writing
Papers for the less authorial,
Great dumb brutes I loved.

# IMPLICATION

Near Chestua in Polk
In a high field at the top
Of a low-crowned mountain, a chain
Drawn through a rusty eye
Summoned me out, and a voice,

Speaking from once lingual
Ground, accosted me as I took
Apples from an autumn tree
As stooped as an old willow,
And left my tracks stepped

Deep in mud by the mouth
Of the open well as I fled the presence
Of implication. On Wilnouty, I found
A trilobitic stone with the look
Of language on it, and in a dry

Biblical county stood like a man
With a slab ordained to be interpreted
To a beleaguered people, but covered
It back with red leaves for safe-
Keeping on the mountain.

At the end of a trail on Whitspur
I came to the runnered house drawn sheer
With the cliff's thousand-foot drop,
And saw through a sliding pane
The Crazy Man reading a book

At his table while behind him
A branch of gum glowed like crown-
Fire in the rough room. I leaned
Close to the glass. *Pascal's
Pensées*, the title said.

I wanted to knock, to be asked in,
To have the din of a word with him:
Inquire what he made of the book,
How the haws were on the pinnacle,
Where there were muscadines.

But I had been warned of intrusion,
Cautioned against interference.  How
Admonition has always persuaded me
To little: to eschew the wild thought,
The errant study: to keep clear

Of implication in a litigious
County filled with quarreling voices
And hateful judgments.  I stormed
The day my friend was shot down on
His doorstone in the presence

Of his wife and children.
"Politics makes enemies," my father said.
"Leave well enough alone."  He strode to the door
And back again and back to the door.
Silhouetted there, he spoke, turning:

"Little landlords sweep with a clean
Broom," he said, meaning more than murder,
His eyes lively with anger.
"Keep your mouth shut, boy.
We have no portion here."

# WINTER

It was only in summer that you became
On especially bright days a wearer
Of shipshape diadems—tight little
Lifeboats of chapeaux crowning seas
Of stark light, adrift from those
Other wide vessels mothers wore:
Milk-white, butter yellow sails
Of daisies, sprigged violets,
Impossibly pink primroses that hawsered
A leghorn brim. I had never seen
The sea, nor had you, but your head
Swam waves like a boat decked with good
Things, chic things, frosted and glazed.
One summer you wore plums and small apples,
Another blue grapes and purple asters.
This was towards fall, and the colors
To me meant mourning. Suspecting, you
Changed to tall pheasant feathers,
Gold and gray and brown, nodding like masts
Over a horizon. My God, *maman*, but you
Could wear a hat! You rarely left
The house in winter. Head wrapped
In a blue shawl, you scattered grain
Among chickens in dim days. It was
As if the flowers dropped guardedly
Underground, the apples and plums
Went soft in dead leaves, grapes
And asters hung dry in the wind,
The golden pheasant clucked deep in
A treehole in the Wild Wood—instead
Of being sheathed in silk paper
On the topmost shelf of the darkest
Closet, where your sails were furled
At the first hint of snow,
Innavigable sea.

# CROPS

The broken crockery she hammered
To bits for her hens, ended up,
Jumbled smooth as beads,
In the eaves of the house.

In those dimpled channels of sand,
Bleached by the drops' pounding,
Pink and blue tablets
Asked to be taken.

When I asked if I should, she said
They had served their purpose already,
And would just slip through
Without curing my curious

Indigestion. Deferring disease,
I put the cold lozenges in my pocket
Where, lying like silk against
My thigh, they lacked even

A hint of rattle. Come Sunday dinner,
I asked for my favorite piece
Of hen: the tough-muscled
Craw, which, she said,

"Is the crop from which your crop
Came," meaning the colored stones,
Which I had liked to suppose
Rained down from the sky.

That day she broke the black pitcher.
Hearing her furious hammer and her call
To the hens, I slid away
To the eaves, thinking

*This will prove it.* I had not yet
Come upon a black stone. But there was
To my astonishment that day
a gold one with a blue flower.

# GRACE

We groaned no thanks
At our ungroaning board.
What we had was ours,
Paid for with blister and cramp.

Our father said,
Gibing at misery,
"We'll eat what there is first
And save what there isn't for later."

Winking at us,
His hungry seven,
Strung to the long bench
Behind the oil-clothed table,

He swilled his cup
Of poor porridge,
Turning the vessel
Upside down at his place,

Signifying
*It is finished.*
I sipped along with my mother,
Amazed at the depth

Of a shallow share.
But I tallied with him.
If God passed by at the road,
I assured myself,

Tonguing the last drop,
Inverting my own cup,
Instead of gaping and groveling,
I'd spit in the sucker's eye.

# PLOUGHING

I push back
through tattered
dictions,
the roughest usage

of tongues,
to the serf's
sniffle of verbs
in the cold shed:

hard consonants,
soft vowels
he hardly
comprehends

for their leniency:
villein's parlance:
ploughshare,
rasp, reaphook,

shovel's bite,
castration device:
the rottenest
eggs of words:

lexicons
of such heavy lives
I could blaspheme
under this mountain:

lacking latin's ivy,
the lilied gloss
of french:
sacerdote,

troubadour:
absurd in my surds:
yet pushing deep
in this black

earth: rolling
grubs of poems out
to the lank
light:

wizened, illiberal,
buttoned into the grave-
clothes of seasonal
joy:

but nonetheless
refunding
the stooping killdeer's
withering cry.

# A DEATH IN THE FAMILY

No respecter of boundaries,
at eight he invaded the domain of bird
and rabbit, slingshot in hand.

I followed, to his bitterness,
he handing me past hedges, through fences,
galloping over fords,

his adoring incubus,
innocent as he of the dread burden of sex,
stuck to his back,

my splashed bottom cold
in the aftermath of his deliberate heels.
Trousers rolled, his brown

stick legs glistening
with the glassy increment of creek,
he plumped me down,

unceremoniously, in green
slathered grass and looked up where
the mad hawk wheeled

and screamed a shrill derision
down at the four-legged creature coming disjoined
in the streamside shade

of the summer willow-line
and the tall wall of earth that kept the rolling
creek from the cornland.

The sling hissed in an arc,
the stone rose high, ineffectually, the hawk
dived as if to seize

the hard brown lump
of my brother's anger, he gritting his teeth
with practical intent

against the dazzling, inter-
secting lines of light, stone, and feathered
body bowing out

of the blue.
His wrath was scriptural, clean, portentous,
magnified by his size.

Brother he was on other days
of heavy glass marbles: cat's eyes, aggies,
milkys, blueys, and water-clear

bubbles twisted with cables
of yellow, red, blue, green, and pokeberry purple
flaring from pole to pole.

"Candy-stripers," he called them.
Ammunition in hand, he went into the great
circular world ring.

I followed,
much to his obvious pleasure, and came out
divested of my small part of

the spinning world's charms,
he snorting laughter at my craft: the taw
ejecting past my cramped thumb

and going off directionless,
like a slippery grape squeezed from its star-
split pouch.

Sniggering, he counted my loss
into the puckered mouth of a Country Gentleman
bag. "You got to knuckle

down," he said.
Home we went then to Mama, the equalizer,
who redivided the spoils.

At eleven, entrepreneur as always,
he went into the rabbit business, constructing
fine traps to wile

the wide-eyes fools,
which always seemed his business. I followed,
making an architecture that sat

floorless on the bare ground
like a slewed chicken box, he grinning, electing
me to farther back fields

because the juxtaposing of my trap
to his would have run down the neighborhood.
He took from his "gums"—

as he nominated them in his own way
with the county speech—fine, flouncing bucks
each morning, I following,

empty-handed, the fat, gutted
flesh bleeding down his thin shoulders.
At thirteen, he took up

the art of the shotgun, his first
casualty being the ceiling of the room where
the gun was laid on peeled

hickory pegs above our parents'
bed. "Damned hammer," he said. "I must have
cocked her on the bedpost."

Dust sifted down through a sifter
of holes, golden, enriched by the sun, onto
his pale, grinning face.

As I remember, he registered
the whole stock of his emotions in full-blown
or incipient laughter,

bitter or joyous,
his whole life long. I followed him still,
cringing at the gun's

thunderous roar until he grew
out of my slower ken, which never included
a gun.

We did not go hunting together
anymore. My books, his bloody hands could
not coincide.

Strangely, he always looked up
to his college-bred brother, not understanding,
you know, but admiring,

and always my staunch defender.
Married at seventeen, he made a poor, almost
beggarly life of his own,

not asking for money or place
but a field to tramp in. And so we went our
diffident, brotherly ways

until, years later, how many
since incredible to tell, he went to his death
while crossing the highway

with a rabbit and a gun,
his face smeared into the concrete under the wheels
of a transport truck.

The undertaker's art improved him,
but we could not touch his face. While he lay
sealed in a face not his own,

I marveled at the shovel hands
stacked on his breast, instruments of all
I had once adored

in his ageless finesse,
the erstwhile slim hands with which he brought
the world to his bidding.

Hounding the coffin where he
bunched in a suit that dwarfed his size,
I could not believe his hands.

Are they real? I wondered,
fitting my family hand to the boxer's gloves.
But nobody answered.

60

They went out of the house
into the strong, rabbit-smelling sunlight,
past the blackberry briars,

across the yellow,
sedge-bound road into the cedars.
I followed.

## LIFE LINE

Begetting us unknowing,
how could they know we
would so proliferate
the worst instances
of their attribution,
gross enough in our gratitude to thank them
even for a button nose,
crossed eyes, a receding
chin, and not above
bragging, for God's sake,
while we proudly practice
our turned-in toes,
of suffering weak lungs
or somebody's gift
of diabetes?

Lying about how we
arrived—woeful non-
swimmers from a dubious
anchorage, floating deltas
at the end of rubbishy,
discharging rivers—how
could they cast loose so
soon our mooring in the
blattering, great, terrible
moment of lightning cracked
across our burning skulls,
and all the skyful of stars
doubled in our eyes?

Dished up on that first
Sunday platter for the un-
believers in all our wet,
crusted beauty, how could we,
when they die, and they all
do it, cry out that they
are leaving us once again
and we not ready, as if

we had not already had
enough of their cruel pranks
and sudden decisions?

But they never dreamed
of us. We look back, gifted
with hindsight and big ears
as our instruments of delving,
and dream of them. How
we gaze into the old photo-
graphs, gasping for their
life's breath!
How we listen
avidly to the twice-told tales
of our brutal parentage!

## II

Of course the place
Is small. I never wanted
More than the comfort
of a close fit: snug
Door, low ceiling:
Approximations of a
Warm embrace. Is it
So depraved, in one who
Took so readily to
Praise, to want so
Much to be enfolded?

# THE TOWN

(*Benton, Polk County, Tennessee*)

No perfect circumference
Inscribed the town,
Of which we were,
Always in transit,

The ragged periphery.
Take a wagonwheel
With spokes lopped off
At different distances

From the hub,
And you get the notion
Of how we were always
Held in dusty

Abeyance,
Down red clay roads,
By the metropolis.
Twelve radii we knew

Before I was grown,
The new house not new
But newly moved into
Being the knob at

The end of farness,
So that we were often,
After a day's evasive journey,
The evening antipodes

Of our morning selves,
Discounting a mile
Or two from the town's
Centrality,

Itself immovable as
A fixed, distracting star,
And we, collectively assembled,
A controlled body

With our own attractive
Shine of sickles gleaming
In the wagonbed,
Jealous new moons of our arcs

Of astronomical wagon
Distances. Only once
Did we pass through the town's
Eye, eyeing

The beautiful striped awning,
The spindly white chairs
In front of the drugstore
With genuine unease

At what the town stood for
In the country preacher's
Incomparable words
Of fallen cities.

Dad whipped up the team,
But not before I spied
The bright-cheeked
Cardboard girl,

Smoking a cigarette
And holding a bottle in
Her moon-white hand,
Leaning in a window.

Then we passed on,
Away from a sunset so red
The whole town seemed on fire
When we looked back.

Even the blue pine wood,
Hung high above the town,
Stood up to its boughs
In underflame.

The bleak holocaust
Of early winter showered the sky
Overhead with charred birds.
We drove on and on.

It was near midnight
When, the fire gone utterly out,
We came to the new place
And unloaded the plows.

# TENANTRY

Always in transit
we were always temporarily
in exile,
each new place seeming
after awhile
and for awhile
our home.

Because no matter
how far we traveled
on the edge of strangeness
in a small county,
the earth ran before us
down red clay roads
blurred with summer dust,
banked with winter mud.
It was the measureable
pleasurable earth
that was home.
Nobody who loved it
could ever be really alien.
Its tough clay, deep loam,
hill rocks, small flowers
were always the signs
of a home-coming.

We wound down through them
to them,
and the house we came to,
whispering with dead hollyhocks
or once in spring
sill-high in daisies,
was unimportant.
Wherever it stood,
it stood in earth,
and the earth welcomed us,
open, gateless,
one place as another.

And each place seemed
after awhile
and for awhile
our home:
because the county
was only a mansion
kind of dwelling
in which there were many
rooms.
We only moved from one
room to another,
getting acquainted
with the whole house.

And always the earth
was the new floor under us,
the blue pinewoods the walls
rising around us,
the windows the openings
in the blue trees
through which we glimpsed,
always farther on,
sometimes beyond the river,
the real wall of the mountain,

in whose shadow
for a little while
we assumed ourselves safe,
secure and comfortable
as happy animals
in an unvisited lair:

which is why perhaps
no house we ever lived in
stood behind a fence,
no door we ever opened
had a key.

It was beautiful like that.
For a little while

# HIWASSEE RIVER

Down there is the river
fresh from the mountain notch,
touched with sulphates from
    the copper veins

in the higher peaks:
shallow, it runs clear: deep,
a blue tinge assesses the truth
    of its origin:

let us go down to
the blue river where it enters
the savannah and green corn grows
    for miles along

flat river bottoms
kept from the river by a hem
of bright green willows:
    let us go down:

the afternoon's gold
light enters the green, is yellow
above the river's bright blue:
    it is time to go:

later, we'll seek
the shallows where spun water
runs and trout swim upstream
    in the cold rushes,

pausing along in the sunshot
eddies over the polished stones, their
stipples red and gold under
    rockbrown shoulders:

we'll take the cow-
path down to the water, follow
the wide laterals cut to fit
    the winding sidehill:

72

we'll move slowly
like the gold jerseys: there  is
no hurry there in the water
        where it idles before

    plunging to deep blue
and the cows drink amiably
at the clean rock edges:
        their stances are calm:

    let us go now:
while the vessel of willows
holds the young water contained
        as in a worked wicker:

    nothing can change:
the afternoon lingers like a warm
hand in the grasp of the current:
        the corn will not

    be drowned, the cornland
will run down to the sunset hill
in slow, drilled hours: *next year*
        the dam will be built.

## THE BROOMERS

They're busy in the high field
That lifts toward heaven, a purple frieze.
The harvest is a stand of sedge

Ready for scything.
It leans from the blade, arched, heavy-headed.
They work upwind.

Back and forth they stroke,
Not round and round as on a still day.
Behind, they lay hands

Of thick straws under the wind,
Making a road they will walk back
Near sundown, tying.

Rumbling down in wagons,
Merchants come with bales of sticky weeding
For the cross-grained floor,

The broomers string to dry
Among the rafters their polished hay.
When the wind roughens

From its autumn flow
Across the low-crowned mountain,
Naked in the mists,

They will twine the straw
In perfect orbits around young hickory poles,
Peeled and knotless

And housewife-yarned
In the strong colors of her duty threads,
To make a sweep to hustle winter by.

## INDIAN SUMMER

It is October in Polk:
Blue pines wheezing, cedars
Shrouding the last light,
The gum tree bruised as an eye.

The tents that once stood here
Are gathered and gone:
Those pointed cities of thongs
Painted orange in the sunset.

Sometimes I find a whistle-bone.
If I could come on amulets!
Instead I walk through buckeyes,
Shagbarks, the spent cones of autumn,

Imagining the red man
Who tainted me with his torment,
His gift a bull-roarer
To frighten devils.

How did I end up like this?
To come, thinking of friends
And their prismatic tongues, to the edge
Of this golden encampment

Of gold hickories gaumed
With shadow, weighing, weighing
Those ancient legmen of hate,
Those bitter warders?

To whom am I responsible
And for what? What is sent down
Is shot like an arrow,
Flung down like a gauntlet.

Rain comes through the gum tree,
Runneling deeper its bruise.  Black
Comes where purple was; a lying voice
Mutters of forgiveness.

I hear the voice as mine.
Yet I was not forgiven for what
I was given.  Here in the rain,
Within earshot of the school,

With pupils singing,
Escaped from the massacre,
I ponder protective covering
From bole and bark, woodsman

Of late, feeling each drop
That falls, each wind that blows.
Coming here, blowing up
These dead fires among

Stone hutches, in dances
Silent as nightfall, chewing
Rosepits and haws, I stand far back
Under branches, waiting a sign.

# NIGHTFALL

Embarked upon a search
with no clue as to what
I was after, I suffered
the sickness of infinitude
along the road of too much
possibility, until I came
at the road's end upon the
house called Mad and learned
to keep my county corner
warm in a corner county.

Which was likely while the
sun shone on field and fern
brake, lovevine and lichen,
earache and apple.  In the rosy
light all voices turned out
friend, all apparitions,
visions.  But there the comfort
ended in a welter of reflected
ease.  I never learned to keep
my head after dark.

# INTERPRETATION

Far on inland
from the river,
which is another boundary,
under the mountain arched like a mitered door
over the lower range,
I stand, angry again
as a brushed bee.

Topped with a dark wood,
the capstone of the county
blocks the sun now
as when I wanted light
deeper than ground level.
What light is there
spews upward from the summit:

Missing, by half, the stones
that float on currents of shadow,
angels without names,
lambs without number.
In the yard of the white church
there is a dark suspension:
ark on black water.

The mountain is a perfect door,
locked against all transgression.
Not even the river forgives
its utter commandment.
Near the river as I passed,
a dark man and his team
were going:

North to the north
star on further, down a lank
furrow fluxed with a dark gleam
and a killdeer crying his withering,
wanting cry.  From withing to withing,
across the river
lay a dead shimmer.

Now that I know those other crossings of meaning,
how sleeveless they are,
how chancy to the personal eye,
I no longer hang
upon the hemlocky lintel
a dazzlement of keys.

## REPRISE

Concession must be made,
Word allowed,
If not of adulation,
Of more modest praise:
How one stood, leaned, sat
Down, took his tobacco,
Spat sideways from a full
Cheek.  Some note must be
Taken of not altogether
Trivial bent: of, if nothing
Else, how his blasphemy
Composed a furious music,
Each malediction arriving
Like a rushed reprise.
My father was a rough
Soul, but I will not let
His life go for nothing.

# III

*Put the books on the floor.*
*These chairs are never*
*Sat in.  Clear a place*
*On the table for the prized*
*Cup, and take care when*
*You walk the narrow paths*
*Of this house.  Reading*
*Was the rede I followed,*
*Finding in the letter*
*The spirit that escapes*
*The law.  I make no apology*
*For weak eyes and a certain*
*Effeminacy of manner.*
*Books engender the androgyne . . .*

*Knowledge is the other*
*Name I chose for love,*
*Though there are doubtless*
*Other fitter names*
*For other fitter men,*
*Come in, dear Kim.  Come*
*In.  Beauty is the utmost*
*Grace of knowing, and I*
*Have posited this house*
*Upon the lean, glazed*
*Stones of grace.*

# AFTERNOON BY THE RIVER

*(For Seamus Heaney)*

My mouth holds round
The soft dove sound
*Ocoee, Ocoee,*
Like puffs discharged

From the valved stack
Of some afternoon
Machine silenced
By distance,

As under the dislodged
Mast of great beeches,
I prospect loam,
Celts, boatstones,

Bird arrows, gnome's
Mud face (where maypops
Still grow in spring)
Till I am sleeved in

Black mold that shelves
Suddenly down
To sulphate water
Under leached mountains

And doves call
Leagues away on
The branch I hold to,
Kneeling down.

# HYPOCRITE MEN

*(In Response to Denise Levertov's poem*
*"Hypocrite Women")*


Hypocrite men, how seldom we speak
of our own doubts, while dubiously
we father woman in her doubt.

And if on Orchard Knob under a tree,
sunlight pouring through green air,
and after love, an amused slip of a girl

told us our pricks are ugly, gone
soft in long foreskins, like an
opossum's crooked bone—why didn't we

admit we have thought so too, and
have since Father Adam? (But what shame?
They are not for the prizer's eye!)

No, they are shy and petulant and ruined:
toy cannon on punctured wheels, peeping
through sandtable hedgerows at the

laughing enemy . . . . and when a dark
drumming fills us, an old child
thrill against the military dark,

we are too much men to
own to such unmanliness.
Masterfully with the psychopomp

we wheedle and play, and beg for
Rapunzel to let down her hair, to
spread it towards us on the pillow,

so that we may pull it to our
cheek and, thumb in mouth, climb
satisfied to sleep. Of course

we say nothing about this in our
report later of how we fought and won.
And our dreams, with what swagger

we translate them into courage
next morning over our cup, winning
all contests again: little boys

sitting along the bridge
above the creek they fished
between cock-rise and cock-shut sun,

dangling their feet above the
fished-out water and handling
the catch: small, white stonefish

gaping for breath: cyclopean minnows
winking and blinking in the perfect
vision of a single eye.

# HANSEL IN OLD AGE

Birds peck the way to safety.
His back grows blue with distance.
But I know his warm heart will change.

"Father!" Sister cries to the signs
Of homecoming ferried now by wings over
The silent treetops. (Step-

Mother, in her house-proud house,
Gloats over him, her most prized possession.)
We walk through brief light

Past high-balling noon into
Sudden darkness, my sister's trembly
Mouth cupping tears, and wake

To an intriguing morning.
In a dell we cannot remember through dreams,
The house stands, iced all

Over with a child's cuisine.
How beautiful the house-proud house is!
From licking the gatepost

To gnawing the cornerstone,
Each act plunges us deeper into predicament.
The house rings with nose-

Pinched laughter. The birds
All say Heh Heh Heh. "Who is laughing?"
Sister asks, pulling a marzipan

Daisy. "Only Stepmother, glad
For our absence," I answer, filling my mouth
With candied marigold. We hide

In a plot of glazed roses. Then
Sprightly on her pretzels, the Old Witch
Waltzes, buttoning her raisin

Eyes into her crusty face.
"You," she says, "have disordered my house.
But, then, how could you resist

My crystaled anomalies?"
Tittering like toast rubbed together, she
Slams the child-swagged gate.

(At home Stepmother brings
Father a red peach on a white plate.)
"Them as are not wanted,"

Remarks our hostess, "want
Who wants them. Come in, my pretties!"
We follow her lead. Among

The hehing birds one clear
Flute note becomes audible. (Father's
Warm heart is changing.) The Old

Witch rings a dangling cherry-
Bob to open the proud, delicious door.
There, in a corner, is

My lemon-barred cage and a broom
With licorice straws for Sister. You all
Know the story by now: how

I fatten on sea foam and Swiss
Chocolate and how my sister and I play
The old lady's game right up

To the oven door, then hurry
Home where Stepmother lies in a carryall
Coffin. Nothing in the mail

Order catalogue, of fruits
Or other comfits, matches the memory.
It is long past now. I have

Searched the woods repeatedly
For a re-vision of the vision. Somewhere,
I know the gingerbread roof

Keeps losing slates to the yard
And the peppermint gate sags on its sugary
Hinges.  Sister sings now

To her own loved brood
In her house over the hill, no longer
Remembering the night

In the wood, the morning waking
To honied wonders.  I stand, looking down
The blue road to the mountain,

Where the trees of autumn
Bloom with colored syrups, watching
My hand raisin with age,

Dreaming of sweet architectures,
Succulent tidbits, and the floury dame
With the incomparable cookies.

# THOMAS JEFFERSON

*(For William Carlos Williams)*

For a beauty to lay beside his own,
Jefferson looked for a gardener
Who could play the flute as well.

It was not news to him that he
Was too beautiful for wilderness,
Wanting music among crab-apples,

In keeping with his proud house
And grand say-so.
Damn his bright head if I

Can forgive his failure to under-
Stand a hickory flute intoning
A virtuous sap is small whistle

To wet in minuets.  He saw what was
Needed and signalled, I think, in
His own divided mind, the right way.

Windfall or worse, the forest was
His, standing and running before him.
But he stopped short of the trees.

Now I labor my point to say
His failure was mine.  I too am
A prince of fashion in a strange land.

89

# DAPHNE

When, to escape him, I reached up
And caught the leaves in my hand,
Among the white-trunked trees
I was no longer visible.

O how in fear I arched there,
My palpitant white limbs rivering
In leaves, one with the windy wood!
And how, worn with running,

He caught his breath in my shade,
Winded with anger, too, and shame.
A god's humiliation hurts.
It was as if I climbed my own branches,

Trunk and rootlet, all, to be gone
From him, and then, like a young girl
Almost persuaded to come down
From tomboy capers and be girl,

Turned in the leaves and, spying
Back on him, saw him take foot, love
Hot in his eyes. Then I fled under
The snowy bark into the heart of the tree.

# ANTAEUS

I am no wrestler of reputation,
Gorgeous in muscle, excellent
In skill of heaving opponents
Down in the dust of the ring,

As at a country carnival,
Planting my feet meanwhile deeper
In the mote heaps of victory
That fly up to be breathed in,

Rekindling my strength at each
High-handed incaution. I am no
Wrestler of reputation bellowing
Invective at the next and the next

Beyond him, out to the edge
Of light, to get ready to hoist
And hurl, and not for reputation only
But for life as well—death being

Decreed the losers—tossing them
One by one into the fecund dust
By grace of rippling thew, down,
Down to ignominious defeat.

I plow my line by the North Star
Out to the edge of light, along the curve
Of the river, by the willow brake
Where no one lurks to challenge

Me, and no one bawls defiance
From the opposite bank to meet him
At the ford. No traveler comes here
Seeking the local apples,

Inquiring direction to what
He is to grapple with. A county Atlas
Would be a county witticism.
I am no wrestler of reputation,

Excellent in heaving skill,
Wearing my gorgeous muscles like
A royal robe, secure in my private
Knowledge.

But until he come (whistling
At the river, seeking reputation)
To wrest my feet clear of the nurturing
Clay and tumble me in air, I will not know

The efficacy of these roots,
The utility of these stones.

# POSTCARD WOODCUT

A man sleeps in the grass.
Overhead, the wind spins the afternoon
Up, upward, to the zenith
Above the gathering storm.

Do they not see him,
The people passing, leaping
Over the dark form in the tossed grass,
Hastening home?

Black trees writhe.  A white spire
Topples.  The tempest runs round.
Carelessly, it meets the runners coming.
The man sleeps on.

It is a good thing for him
There to be sleeping, to be dreaming
There, while the people flee
Into the purple evening.

# NOONING

(*An exercise poem after William Carlos Williams' "Fine Work with Pitch and Copper."*)

Now they are resting
in heat-moted light
under the balm tree

hunkered about
like the small cocks
they will magnify

to headtall stacks
pale as pulled candy
after the lunch

The scent of bleeding
timothy is in their bread
Along the meadow

windrows crawl
in the slow wrinkles
of stockponds

Set stakes march
in file downfield
One picks his teeth

one sucks a stem
one pisses at the edge
of shade

One still chewing
takes up a splayed fork
and strums its tines

# INTRUDER

(For Jorge Luis Borges)

Walking in a wood,
I heard a sound
That clanged in a clearing,
And went in.

My shadow followed,
Prancing before me.
(Good dog, my shadow.)
The air dazzled and rang.

Two knives were fighting
With aplomb and finesse,
Suspended in mid-air
Like crystal spurs

On clear ozonic cocks.
O how they glared.
Under them the red leaves
Shuffled and danced

As if turned
By accustomed feet
Executing a perfectly
Attuned will.

Alarmed, my shadow
Backed, howling, and fled,
I, hackled, in front.
But not before one

Blade, flashing, swept.
The other fell down
And lay as a still
Demolished point

For the other's eye.
But lay impatiently,
Wanting up again.
Knives have nine lives,

The trees whispered.
A leaf sailed by
And touched my shoulder,
Falling that much

Before my time.
My shadow bawled,
Shamelessly at variance
With manlier logic.

And we both ran on
To the wood's far edge,
Arrant believers.
(Good show, my shadow!)

# ADDRESS

Cornets and bugles
And throbbing drums:
Ah, Rilke!
I understood these once
From a boxful of toys
Owned by another boy.

I, too, would like swans.
But this is crow country,
Mr. Yeats:
At best a place of killdeers
Crying their withering,
Wanting cry.

Seamus Heaney,
The smell of dead men's blood
In barnyards must be heady
But is past imagining,
I have not been made to know
Politics that well.

We do have a thorn tree here.
But if we are careful,
We can step among the old spikes
And gather the leathery
Luscious pods
That are not like honey.

# IV

The way a man hangs
A blue hat on a yellow
Wall, and makes an art
Thereby, is, after all,
The way an art grows
In official clothes
To guard a cornfield.
That I choose now
To stuff a greater abstract
Does not make me a strange
Being by virtue of my
Other vices . . .
It is, of course, only
An adopted habit of mind.
Too engrossed in convoluted
Things to think straight,
I am, as it were, engulfed
By corals, cabbages, and
The deep hearts of cyclonic
Flowers, as well as the
Swirls and eddies of the
Humped, riverine brain,
On whose topography the mind
Is so tremulously posited.

# DAY'S END

Above the sedge-spiked graves
the red-shouldered hawk
spirals downward,
screaming.

A gray rabbit creeps under
my father's bushy name
and becomes a part
of the still stone.

In the red light,
straddling the stone lamb,
the hawk burns,
dissatisfied;
then he grave-hops
to the head
of a broken angel.

I feel his talons grip
my own eyeballs.

The rabbit sticks to the stone.
Only his muzzle moves
at a meal of small grass.

(O father, protect him from
the edicts of the Father!)

When the hawk screams again,
he is high up
and flame-colored,
circling the cooling thicket.

It is near sundown
and time for me to empty
the fat black berries
and wash the pail.

The red cow has already
preceded me along the spindling
hill-path home.

# TROLL POEM

### I.

The door to the root cellar
stands half-way open.
The tools I need,
the fork, the great engaging shovel,
lean against the slant wall.

A potato lies,
suspiciously toothed,
brown as a paper sack
on the gray dirt floor.

I need to go in.
But have been promised,
among other things,
a meeting with God.

I am too shameless
even for my own
abiding sense of shame.

Who will have the tools
will have the door.
It is the angle the door makes
with the gray wall
that intrigues me.

### II.

I met trolls once
in the gray beechwood
coming out of trapdoors
in the spoon-dropped moss.

Rooty brown men
with oily eyes
like blue woods' springs
with buried trees in them.

When they laughed,
mirth shifted in their mouths
like the partial neighs
of misbegotten horses.

Sometimes any door will do.

### III.

"I'm pleased to meet you,"
said the chief troll, limp-leering,
his face like a brown-ink
horror drawing
left out in the rain.

"You know me, neighbor.
Now what of your own
bedazzled identity?"

He leaned in the window.
"I know you from trolls.
I know you from God.
God is not father
except in a minute and planetary way.
Trolls are my kin,
intimate as cousins,
raised like potatoes
from the dust of the ground.
You shine in the house,
I shift in the cellar.
A spatulate mole
makes a fine companion.
Help me with you.
Give me three guesses.

"Who calls you 'son'?
Is your name enough?
What is the wind's word
in the maze of your earhole?"

IV.

I know my father.
I know my mother.

He's in the wood,
drinking a flame
from the cup of his hands,
lacing the simple blue
with a chord of fire.

She's in the house
turning an apple
on the spit of her love.

I have only to close
the cellar door
to know who I am,
or open it wide
to answer your questions:
the simplest way's
to destroy the angle
the door makes
with the gray wall.

V.

A rare doom color
like ink and milk fusing
in a cup of water
lights the prospect.
It is the weather
of more northern epics,
morning feats
in epic blue,

in which my father's hands,
gold in the apple flesh
as a woodsman's tent
suddenly shimmering with fire,
reach and go out.

A star plunges.

Stars are incidental
because essential.
It is the hands, young man,
epically boned and melded,
that lightly handle the doom
alive in the lilac world.

Dawn blows across the wood.

## VI.

In eye-dropper light
spent waiting between
the facing lilac,
the burgeoning gold
of flowers peering west
the night before,
I travel as far
as a pearl button
on the slack belly
of my blue shirt . . .

while in a paralyzed
high noon field
yet to be shone upon
a human stonehenge
wades its shadow
of motive and master.

Hello hello hello!
Trains are essential
because incidental.

One might as well
cry real tears
or toss a ball
over handy housetops
with no one catching
as ask those stones
their human meaning.

# CALLIGRAPHY

I had expected the lettering to carry
A date of some kind: of gift or purchase.
But this fine Spencerian hand is more

A line in a copybook, a splendid practice.
*Joseph Leander McDowell*, I read in wonder
of deft calligraphy, and then, much as an

After-thought, *Benton, Tennessee*, as if
The medico from North Carolina found place
Less significant than his sounding name—

Its own geography of places.  Where now is
The title *Doctor* my mother said he strove
So mightily for?  It is not here.

Inside the leather-covered box the shine
Of blue velvet is undimmed; the stethoscope
Is frozen though, curled like the fossil

Beat of all the hearts he listened to.
The metal shines unburnished.  Things last in
Unexpected ways.  These were my progenitor's.

That should be satisfying enough.  But it is
Not.  I need more than a ticked box from a man who
Swam leagues of mountain inland from the Cape

To reach me but did not arrive, drowning before
In some interim valley, the letter unwritten,
The poem I am told he was capable of, unpenned.

Classic swimmer, son of the dark stranger,
Whose ecclesiastical first name does not tidy
Up matters: grandfather: I need more.

A beetling sermon would do, some rules copied
Out for classroom conduct, numbered paradigms
For shy, reluctant scholars: anything would do.

In another poem I cheated, putting fine, false
Words into his mouth from pride, words he would have
Known, knowing *Sibylline*, my mother said.

This poem is true.  An artful script then is all
I have to speak to—beside which my own crabbed hand
Is mazed as sparrow tracks in smudged snow.

*Dazer of crowds, metaphor man, I need more than*
*A failed comparison to be custodian of.  Damn it, Grandpa,*
*Your bantling carelessness breeds a family ire.*

# LUNA MOTH

The ghost of a great
green fly trailing
the moonlight

drifts in the shadow
like a pale human
swimmer standing

high out of some
dark water.  Nightly,
on my bright mother

quilt, I lie down
in the dark valley,
my head cradled

lovingly in
the crook of my arm.
The green grass grows

all around, all
around.  Over me, the
passing stars,

those bright,
casual haberdashers,
button me

nightly
into my
graveclothes.

# NOCTURNE: SPRINGTIME

The moon moves downhill towards morning;
The dark mountain soars like a black wind,
So high the last white cloud goes out.

How many nights have I dreamed you
In fragments, pieces of faces, scraps,
Splinters of desire, O you ungettable
Compound! How many nights
From the assembly line of love
Selected parts only to fool the pattern!
Aware of you not as a vector of any
Time or place, scintilla of a golden
Kingdom (but only as I would remember
Laughter about lips that no longer
Laugh, imprinting with my own
The salty shadow!), I cannot distinguish
You from all the oddments of a crowded year.
At least not here, not now.
My ordered love terminates in wild
Disorder, the formal time is past.
But your demesne defines this nightly
Neighborhood, your young grove leaps
Behind some hill. But when I walk
Among the trees where love once startled
And fled, a wild phantasmal shoot is
Your plantation. I idle in the underglow
Of sad naked glaucous stems resplendent
In purple darkness, feeling gothic,
Myself wearing a lilac musk darker
Than the strong shade shading the water trees.

This is my particular memory of you:
These strong withes rising like gray flame
From violet burning are the tree-borne grass
In which I see the eyes no longer looking,
The tree-tall grass in which I am afraid
(Young dreamer, old in time, seeking
Entelechies!), the moleskin grass

Softer than the first streaming violet,
In which resides the dry crackling garment
Still worked with that faint design
I touch with dread (the old inhabitant
Lies far away in mottled gold!).
You have receded into landscapes, diminished
To eye-bearing tree, hair-fern, lipped flower.
Your voice quickens elsewhere in the folded land.
I always lose you there,
Between the night and the morning,
In the green, remembered, flowing earth.

I pass the graveyard, going home.
Old leaves are blowing in the dark roadway.
I think I hear weeping:
Children are having a funeral for a dead bird.
My dream burns out with light,
And I, the night's compositor,
Turn bleakly to the room where sleep is born
And a man dies among his own lilies,
Himself chief mourner.

## OLD THOMAS

The old man there
whose right cheek keeps trying
to jump over his left eye
told me in my asking days
to read a poem each morning
if I cared to be viable,
have a resilient heart.
I believed,
and read a poem a day
sure as sunrise
and came to nothing much
but a succession of poems,
a procession of days.
I know now succession
is not success.
Being old is what it is
and getting ready for a procession,
heart dry as a skinned leaf.
But I still read my daily poem
and curse roundly the stupid poets
I am so addicted to.
Not that I really hate *them*.
I hate *him*
the silly old man
who should have known poets
know nothing
and can help nobody,
not even themselves.
These days,
past wisdom and counsel,
aggravated by advice,
he sits in a sunny corner of my yard,
concerned only with the orchestration
of his own gusty bowels.
He farts like tearing brown paper.
God, how I despise his windage
interrupting my poem!
I should have got more out of him
than just a habit

and an acrobatic left cheek
that keeps trying to broad-
jump my right eye,
I keep telling myself,
hearing my own stiff belly growl
under the poetry book
like a starved hound hunting
a paper wood
with a cold muzzle.

# BREAKFAST

After having run all night
in place
to escape the Terror,
I watch while the toast burns
the upstreet jock jog down
to keep his genitals
alive and well.

While in the neighbor's tree—
pale yellow tree,
lemony tree,
soft as damp silk in autumn—
the peacock screams just once
and shows its ass,
its beautiful scrumptious ass,
to the morning stars.

The jock pauses
to take an amazed long piss
under that stunning tower of silk,
that more stunning erection
that rattles down
in the gingko tree
as he unearths from his strap
in the gold-filled light
a pale lanky prick
that might have been the other end
of a white drawstring,
and runs on.

Then I eat my black bread
and lick my ebony fingers,
knowing at least two carbon-
dated knowledges:
one—that day after night
in our raging dream
we all go utterly mad;
and, two, that any deaths we die
in a multiplicity of hereafters
will be purely posthumous.

# THE OLD MAN

Confusion covers the old man like sleep.
Never quite clear, never wholly awake,
He drowses through connections.  Softest
Ties knot together hardest realities.
O I am envious to see feathers fly
Iron weights of fact between them,
Bright leaves fall upward, cry of birth
Translate to last soft mewl of dying.
Between hour and hour, dream and dream,
Twilight and false dawn, down
Is the vector muscle.  O soft, softly,
In softness, the day turns under the news,
And he wakes smiling among the communiques,
Knowing his death is already posthumous,
Knowing the only truth is survival.

# UNWANTED CHILDREN ON THIS WANTED HILL

Unwanted children on this wanted hill,
Breaking the grape-blue trees at peep of day,
O be thou wanted by a fiercer will.

You meek ones know audacity is still
In quietness, and *yes* is all you say,
Unwanted children on this wanted hill.

You harsh ones persevere in strictness till
The last grapes fall like shot and, homing, may
Be wanted truly by a fiercer will.

You ribalds come in mother-wit to spill
With jesting shame, and scorn the game you play:
Unwanted children on a wanted hill.

But you are not the bitter lot who kill
The morning's image with their wrathful way,
Being unwanted by a fiercer will.

At peep of day, ransacking frosty swill
High in the autumn trees that creak and sway,
Unwanted children on this wanted hill,
O be thou wanted by a fiercer will.

# BIRTHDAY POEM

Now it is October, and the coat is comfortable,
The lapel worn through from too much grasping and leaning

And pondering down. It is a preferred attitude,
Has a wise look to it, is even distinguished, if one

Accepts posture, a leaning down, as distinction.
Strange that gazing to heaven is never a sign of wisdom.

It is the stance of saints instead, of mutes,
Idiots blind to all but emblazoned glories, flamboyants

Who adore flame. It is October, and the cut
Of your coat is so deftly accustomed, and you, in it,

So likewise accustomed, having assumed all roles,
Spoken all parts. But once past the harvest moon, you knew

The days fell down and down. As well you knew
The moon slid and the stars, as suddenly as light leaps

Over a wall and shadows embrown the still
Warm side. It was not and is not wisdom, only a quick

Perception that flees. You are aware only of
Warmth still and are still comfortable with leaning.

You stand in the shadow of the wall, only a
Little more hunched than you were before, contemplating

A red wrist, a nail like a blue eye: a little
More studious, if gravity signs. It is your birthday.

## SMALL POEM

Walking
the paths of his own
premise

fixing the right word
daily nail-like into
its post

speaking exactly
crossbar and
beam

living with
utmost precision

a man could
eventually go away
without leaving.

## little old man

sleeping he's
slack but
contained

in his chair
ungainliness
disallowed

by his dolly
size only if
he were

larger would
one begin to
contemn him

for lolling
open-mouthed
with drops

of clear spittle
pulling like
small crystal

pears from
underlip
marble pink

in ear and
chin lobe
and pharynx

translucent
he shines away
flies

in air of
chewed mint
what

he is
is pure wrong
dimension

for corruption
as if the world
seeing

said see
carefully to this
child

## a septuagenarian watching a ladybug
## on his arm addresses his

old body
bole of my soul
host

to fungus
ladybug
indurated rivulet

of vein
dry-rot
peel

scale
stain
iodine-spotted

like ticks
all over
you've grown so

arboreal
that
considering

the newest
rosette
spreading

at the end
of my nose
i shouldn't wonder

anytime now
to hear a
treefrog

piping
in the scruffy
knothole of my ear

# VIEWPOINT

From where I sit, I see
A trivium of roads,
A bivium of rivers,
An intersection of mountains:

In between, wild hedges map
The small farms into gatherings
Of young corn and grasses.
From a flower-starred meadow

Fringed with blue pines,
Someone flies a blue kite
Against steamy white clouds
As clean as the church

On its sunlit knoll
In the middle distance.
Near to the church, half-
Hidden in shade,

One low, bent stone
Winks like a water-drop
Caught in green leaves
After sudden rain.

All morning I've read a book
In this upland pasture
Between a river and a mountain,
At the end of one road,

The beginning of another,
Liking the angle the land makes,
While close by a rose hoists itself
Up a staghorn sumac,

Contriving candelabra—
Which is only to say
That a poet needs to get under
His own light.

# OLD MAN HILL-CLIMBING
## ON SUNDAY

The horizon hangs here
Like scalloped cloths:
Beyond the first, another
Hangs in the hard notches.

Between the two—
I can see no farther
In a land lapped
As a snakeskin is—

The weather gets caught
In juts and precipices,
Warped, interstitial,
But always coming.

A busy little river
Falls in and out:
Down truncated meadows
Its intermittent gleam

Cozens the eye.  Above
Are cliffs and crowded
Trunks deep in ancient mast,
And a sudden spill of quartz

In an interface of clay.
Here is either up or down.
The sun sails clear only
At noon, and twelve o'clock

Is dead center of light.
I have climbed slopes and
Huckled them down all morning:
At the lip of a  bluff, pause,

Out of breath and close
To out of living.  Every rock
Is here limbate with green.
Spoonbread moss hummocks

Root and horizontal ground
Bough.  Tall poplars slim
Their way out of scabbed
Oak and penciled pine,

Powdered breastworks
Of great chestnuts lie down-
Hill, and the memory of burs
Quickens to buckeyes.

# AT THE DOOR

The red bitch stretches.
Her red tongue laps out,
Languishing.
She bellies the dust,
By it made whole.

She is consigned
To the grind of the doorstone
But not to the dust
Of more precious savor
Which will release a thing

As the savor of nutmeg
Floats free from the brown meal
Of its strength,
The secret broken,
Not dust entire.

Limbs are in motion
Towards the self of limbs
By the self's scruple:
Line and double
Line arriving:

Plumb and plummet both,
Both hemming and hawing,
Harrowing and hymning,
Resuming in flowers
Daylong

The bolting of dust:
A finer essence.
When the soul occurs
Like a gifted topknot,
Like a reeking fugue

From the roof of Sunday,
Bellying the ground,
Red tongue lapping,
The red bitch rolls
And stops and watches.

## APRIL SHOWERS

This was to have been a day
of great slow motion,
time stilled in the rain

to the utmost step
that admits procession
into the perfect circumstance,

under the bent heads,
the soft, examining voices.
Among the damp, flat-topped daisies

this was to have been
a close-veiled day, a day of low
full clouds scudding against

blue half-mountains.
But the tilted meadow
has already brightened,

suddenly the clouds have lifted.
Far ahead, on the knoll
apexing our destination,

white stones are glimmering
with an excess of light.
Steps quicken up the pathway.

Keeping to the measured tread,
I cannot match the new pace
up to the ring of exotic flowers.

So I fall out onto the grass,
already sick with the fancied stench
of hot carnations.  Besides,

this was to have been a few-
worded day, a day of dull
surfaces, duller

adulations unexposed
in all the quicksilver nature
of praise.

That I was prepared for.
This I might have prepared for.
But one preparation is enough.

I am not ready yet
for the totally unexpected sunlight
smiling on all the ornaments.

# SMALL SUNDAY MORNING POEM

On a good big boat
of river rock
moored in flood time
at center field,
under church-white clouds
and a kite-blue mountain,
among endlessly
repeated flat-
topped daisies,

I sit, holding
a string tethering an
invisible windy tug
that might well be
the mountain pulling,
hearing the speaker
roundly declare
through an open window
and a blossoming frieze
at the wood's edge

that the heart of the matter
and the matter of the heart
are one and the same,
his voice as seamless
as the Sunday flowers,
devoid of sense
as my easy mind
indulging itself
in the blessed assurance
of the man who flies
a sky-blue kite
in October.

# THOUGH I DO NOT BELIEVE

Though I do not believe
And a few bells tolling
In God the Father
In God the Father's Son
Nor that Other Emissary
Spooky as milkweed down
And do not expect
To be lifted up
From the floor of being
Any further than
A mouse is
I am not afraid
I am not afraid
To be dust
Gentle and brown
Gentle and brown
At the root of things
Lilies and wheat
Lilies and wheat
Onions that grow
Into the fire
Of a man's hot tongue
Sharply speaking
Words of the angels
Whose glittering scales
String the field
In mirrors of mica
To the rim of the river
Where the dusty earth
Was once exclaimed
From my timorous soul
I am not afraid
I am not afraid
Hear my declaration
Here by the animal run
Where the walk is exquisite
The dance is exquisite
The skip is exquisite
The leap is exquisite

Down to the water
Murmuring by
The red clay road
Rut deep in river
I am not afraid
To mix my dust
With the dust of these
With the dust of these other
Sleek lovely ones
Whose mire I cannot
Reasonably exceed
And all transfused
Into the dust
Gentle and brown
Gentle and brown
At the root of things
The glaze of lilies
The gloze of wheat
The fire of onions
Speaking sharply
The words of angels
On a man's hot tongue
In which I do not either
Much believe
Though wings are singing
Above the river
Runing crystal
Shoaling white
Increasing blue
But for which I thank Thee
For understood reasons
Thou It of Things
So variously named
So curiously called
God the Father
God the Father's Son
God the Father's Other Emissary
Spooky as milkweed down
As a dandelion's uneasy head
Exploded by pouting lips
On the mystery of wind

# DESIDERATUM

I search always for a room
    in which all things matter greatly
        and equally:

To enter which I leave outside
    the isotropic door all manner of instruments
        of calibration,

All gyres and springes, all traps
    and pitfalls inherent in the nature
        of measurement,

Except the catoptric glass
    a man needs for mirroring the image
        of his own serenity:

That caprifig hung in the slow,
    reluctant branches to hasten flowers
        to willingness,

Perfumed catalyst charming
    the wasp to work its flickering,
        fiddling charm:

That is, the whole heart,
    honest as the equiparent fullness
        of the emptiest

Habitational dream:
    for across that threshold is love,
        that perfectly pure space

Where no dimensions are given.
    Bodies are not needed to describe
        the things in that room,

From the shelves and ledges
    of which is reflected only the amiable,
        and uncritical, soul.

# MY BROTHERS

*(After the Spanish [Mexico] by Marco Antonio Campos)*

My brothers left bit by bit,
Not one by one, as brothers
Usually leave.  They left a little
Each day so that I no longer
Recognized them.  On their
Backs they carried the wind,
Country women, the red road,
The most fancied of rewards
But never childhood.
What did I do meanwhile?
What the deuce did I do?
I began to draw in cheap tablets
The most handsome of men,
Who had orgasms only in my poems.
My life hid itself successfully
In books, unlived.
I distrusted love,
Mistreated friendship,
Misunderstood experience.
I existed unseen, among
Idiots and, what is worse,
The eternally innocent.
Print washes the guilty
Whiter than snow,
Even when the sin is mind.
For lack of living,
I invented life.
For lack of a father,
I remained a child.
For lack of a child,
I am an unfinished house
Fallen into ruin.

This, then, is my
Checkered dwelling, Kim,
My piecemeal place.
Patched with ghosts a close
Celebration wraps me in.
All things are signed here
With the personal graffiti
Of love . . .
Love, too, is happenstance,
Though such interiors as
Mine are not as accidental
As they seem.

Come in, Brother.  Because
I love you, I have spent my
Life trying to teach you
Two things:  How to let a
Brother live as he will
And die his own way:
Two things which are only
One in the end.  We are old now.
Must I still plead my obstinate
Case with you?  Let us once
More share the thin gleanings.
In the presence of painted
Ladies, old souls, and tribal
Laser eyes, who can say what
Is the best nature
Of love?

# ACKNOWLEDGEMENTS

The publisher acknowledges with appreciation the generosity of the following in allowing the inclusion here of poems originally published by them:

APPALACHIAN JOURNAL: *The Game; The Sharer; Grace*
BLACK WARRIOR REVIEW: *Viewpoint*
CREEPING BENT: At the Door; *Bedbugs*
CUMBERLAND POETRY REVIEW: *Postcard Woodcut*
HOG'S HEAD REVIEW: *Interpretation*
MOSSY CREEK JOURNAL: *Hiwassee River*
NATIONAL FORUM: *Life Line; Small Sunday Morning Poem*
OLD HICKORY REVIEW: *My Brothers*
POETRY NOW: *Winter*
PRACTICES OF THE WIND: *The Mantelpiece*
RACCOON: *The Broomers*
SATURDAY REVIEW: *Thomas Jefferson*
SEWANEE REVIEW: *Summer Revival: Brush Arbor; Summer; Ploughing; Nocturne: Springtime*
SOUTHERN POETRY REVIEW: *Daddy, You Bastard; Desideratum*
THE SMALL FARM: *A Death in the Family*
SPIRIT: *Indian Summer; Afternoon By The River; Hansel In Old Age; Address*
VANDERBILT POETRY REVIEW: April Showers
VOICES: *Daphne; Moving Day; Troll Poem*
ZONE III: *Leathers; Nooning; Invitation To Kim; Early Autumn; The Mill On The Chestua; Schoolhouse Hill; Antaeus; Calligraphy; Old Man Hill-Climbing On Sunday*